YESTERDAY'S CHILDREN

a photographic essay by
Patricia Worth Simmons

Personal Acknowledgments

First, I wish to thank my husband, Bill, for the encouragement he gave me and especially for his interest and help in the preparation of the manuscript and all which that involved. I also wish to thank my father for his continued support and for all those friends who believed in me all along.

I wish to express appreciation to all those people I interviewed and to all those whom I photographed. Specifically, I wish to thank Mrs. Frances Eyster, Washington D. C.; Mr. and Mrs. Milo Sterritt, Mesa, Arizona; Mrs. Jessie Williams, Auburn, Alabama; Mrs. Burton and the Butler Senior Citizens, Bloomington, Indiana; Mrs. Flick and the Crestmont Senior Citizens, Bloomington, Indiana; and Mrs. Sciscoe, Bloomington, Indiana.

Notes

There is no connection between the people in the photographs and the matching quotations.

* * *

This book attempts to present the experience of old age from the older person's viewpoint, and all the quotations in the book are selected from interviews with older people.

Acknowledgments

The following pages from *Yesterday's Children* contain quotations or adaptations from quotations from the indicated references.

Pages 4 (. . . should not consider yourself old as long as your faculties and way of thinking are reasonable), 16, 38, 60, 62, 64, 70, 72, 76, 80, 90, 124, 158, 202 (The older people grow and the closer they get to dying, the more likely they are to take up religion. They get too old to sin, so they take up religion), 212, 216, 230, 235, 247 are from:

Clark, Margaret and Barbara Anderson, *Culture and Aging*. Springfield, Illinois: Charles C. Thomas, 1967, pages 60, 61, 62, 119, 55, 120, 63, 239, 269, 66, 251, 51, 65, 307, 268, 201, 199, 177 and 229 respectively.

Pages 4 (When you look backward more than you look ahead, that's a sure sign of old age) and 88.

Cabot, Natalie Harris, *You Can't Count on Dying*. Boston: Houghton Mifflin Co., 1961, pages 233 and 63, respectively.

Pages 130, 208, 224.

Cumming, Elaine and William E. Henry, *Growing Old*. New York: Basic Books, 1961, pages 183, 209, 196, respectively.

Page 14.

Hansen, Percy M. *Never too Late to be Young*. New York: F. Fell, 1966, page 89.

Pages 34, 42, 94, 146, 202. (My religious beliefs have made my older years happy).

Hunter, Woodrow Wilson and Helen Maurice, *Older People Tell Their Story*. Ann Arbor: University of Michigan Institute for Human Adjustment, Division of Gerontology, 1953, pages 23, 59, 50, 45, and 65, respectively.

Pages 66, 86.

Havighurst, Robert J. and Ruth Albrech, *Older People*. New York: Longmans, Green and Co., pages 62, and 155, respectively.

Pages 6, 22, 32, 74, 196, and 232.

Reichard, Susanne, and Florine Livson and Paul G. Peterson, *Aging and Personality: A Study of 87 Older Men*. New York: John Wiley and Sons, 1962, pages 127, 86, 131, 127, 39, and 154, respectively.

Pages 28 and 68.

Rose, Arnold Marshall and Warren A. Peterson, *Older People and Their Social World*. Philadelphia: F. A. Davis Co., 1965, in article, "The 'Retired' Stamp Collector: Economic and Other Functions of a Systematized Leisure Activity," by Edwin A. Christ, page 105.

Pages 15, 216, and 260.

Scott-Maxwell, Florida. Article is in Clark, Margaret and Barbara Anderson, *Culture and Aging*. Sprinfield, Illinois: Charles C. Thomas, 1967, page 435. It is an abridged radio talk first delivered on the Third Programme of the British Broadcasting Corporation. Shortly thereafter, it was printed in the pages of *The Listener* (LII: 1337, October 14, 1954, pp. 627–9). It was later reprinted in *Harper's Bazaar* in an article entitled, "We are the Sum of Our Days."

Pages 112 and 144.

Townsend, Peter. *Family Life and Old People*. London: Routledge and K. Paul, 1957, pages 174 and 147 respectively.

For
Mrs. John H. Hanson

Preface

This book presents the experiences of the older citizens of our country. The text speaks of their troubles and their joys in their own words, and the photographs eloquently capture the pleasure and the poignancy of their lives. It is not so much a story of a single group of people at a certain age as it is a picture of the experiences which all humanity share. If there is any single pervasive theme to the book it is that all the ages of Man are united by the same enjoyments of companionship, family, and social activity, and that all the ages of Man are subject to the same desperate fears about money, loneliness, and illness. The pages of this book portray an understanding of life which is common to older and younger people alike. It demonstrates the unity of Man in all his variation, in all his failures, and all his successes. It is a book about Man.

Older citizens, however, also have experiences which are unique. While it is true that people of all ages face the possibility of death daily, older people are particularly aware of the transient quality of life. The intimacy of old age and death has led many people to attempt to ignore its existence. Old age is avoided as if it were death itself, rather than an integral, important and lengthy period of *life*. It is a part of life which could be more rewarding, if it were only more highly esteemed.

David Pryor, M. C.

Contents

Part I 13

Part II 151

Part III 191

Part IV 233

PROLOGUE:

How Old Is Old?

"You're just as old as you feel."

"You're just as old as you feel."

"When you look backward more than you look ahead, that's a sure sign of old age."

"A person is old when they get narrow minded. They don't consider anybody but themselves. After you talk with a person awhile, you usually can tell if they're old."

"You should not consider yourself old as long as your faculties and way of thinking are reasonable."

"You're just as old as you feel."

"I think a lot of it is the way old people dress themselves; that's what makes them old."

"If I don't stop drinking, I will be old. It makes you older. I've seen men look about sixty when they're forty."

9

"Old age is when it gets so you have to sit all day. People don't care for you when you're old."

"When you get older, you wish you were younger."

"Old people are goofy to a certain extent because they are afraid to gamble. They're more secure than the youngster."

"When you get so-called old, you never feel like you're that old. Everybody else is old, but you're not. Everybody's old but me. That's how I feel."

"When you're old, the young ones look much younger than they are."

"The biggest damned fools are the old folks. I have no offspring to make a fool of me."

PART I

"I get sick and tired of all of this talk about senior citizens and the golden age group. I am not a senior citizen. I am Mrs. G. Cooper, and I will be Mrs. G. Cooper until I die. I do my own work. I take care of my husband, and we are not on charity. I don't want to be placed on the shelf just because I am over sixty years of age, and I do not intend to be. I would like to punch the nose of the next person who refers to me as a senior citizen."

"What we get is an odd experience of anonymity, as though we moved along the cracks between the lives of other people."

"You first begin to realize you're getting older when you look in the mirror and see all the wrinkles."

"I hate to look in the mirror. I see changes, and I'm not happy about it. I try to stay as I am. Nine times out of ten, I'm not pleased with myself. I'd like to stay as young as I am."

"People say that my wrinkles make me look distinguished."

"Time sort of wrecks our appearance. You wouldn't think I used to be redheaded. I was, and I don't think I was so bad lookin'. Now I'm a bad lookin' critter. I'm self conscious; that's it. When I first got gray hairs, I used to pull 'em out. Didn't help a bit, not that first bit."

"When you have to retire, you suddenly realize that you are at the end of the line. You begin to wonder what it's all about. But after you get into the swing of retired life, you find out there's more to life than trying to eke out a living."

"This is the best life I ever had. It's an easy life. You don't have to worry about anything. You can just poke around; sleep when you're sleepy, eat when you're hungry, swim whenever you want, and do what you want."

"After you retire, you have to become acquainted with each other again. For so many years you've lived in two separate worlds."

"It was quite hard getting used to my husband being at home all the time, very hard to get adjusted to that. It just seemed like, if I wanted to go ahead and do something, I had to stop in the middle of it. Maybe I'd had to fix lunch, and if he wasn't home, I wouldn't have to do that. I could finish what I was doing.

"You know how it is when a man's gone from eight to five, six days a week, and suddenly he's planked right down in the middle of you. A woman's work goes on whether she's retired or not."

"I feel that in a retirement area the people are closer together than they are back home. When you're back home, why you get in a bus to go to work and you sit there. You sit there, and you don't talk to them unless you meet somebody you know. I think when a person is older, if they can afford it, they're much better off in a retirement area."

"We looked that place over, and my wife, she said, they could just as well name it 'cemetery city.'" They got houses row on row like tombstones in a churchyard, for the old folks. We want to live the way we always lived, not in some damn colony where you wait to get pushed over the fence."

"Just sittin' around and doing nothin',
I think that's the worst thing that happens
to retired people."

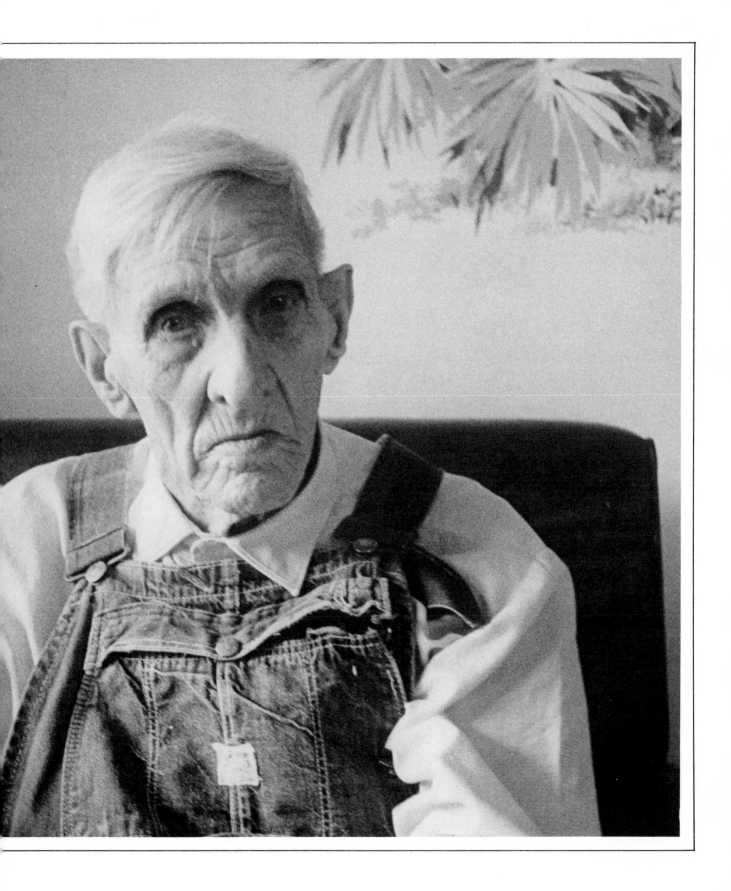

"Anybody that's worked hard all their lives and are worn out from their work would naturally want to retire so they can rest."

33

"I was born to work. I'll never retire."

"Retiring is like putting nails in your coffin."

"When I see all those younger men at the employment office, I can tell that an old man like me doesn't have much of a chance to get work."

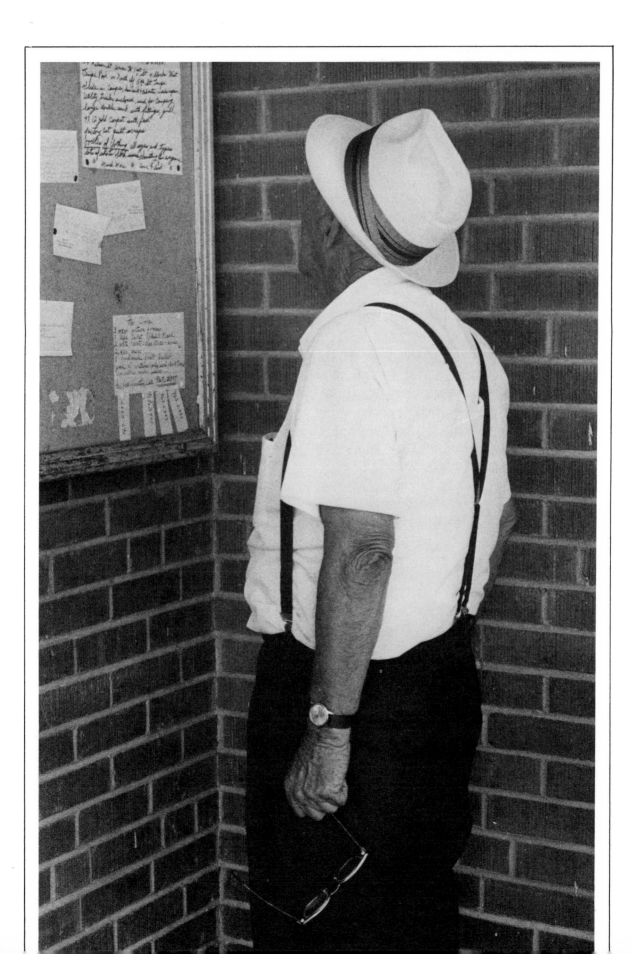

"When you're older, you don't get out and work. You can't work. Nobody wants to hire you. Like they figure old people can't do the work like a younger person. In my idea, I think the old person does better than the young people, cause the older people will stay on the job and do the jobs like they supposed to be done. The younger people, they go in and work and make one or two paydays, and they up and gone."

"To make a living, I have to use all my time sewing."

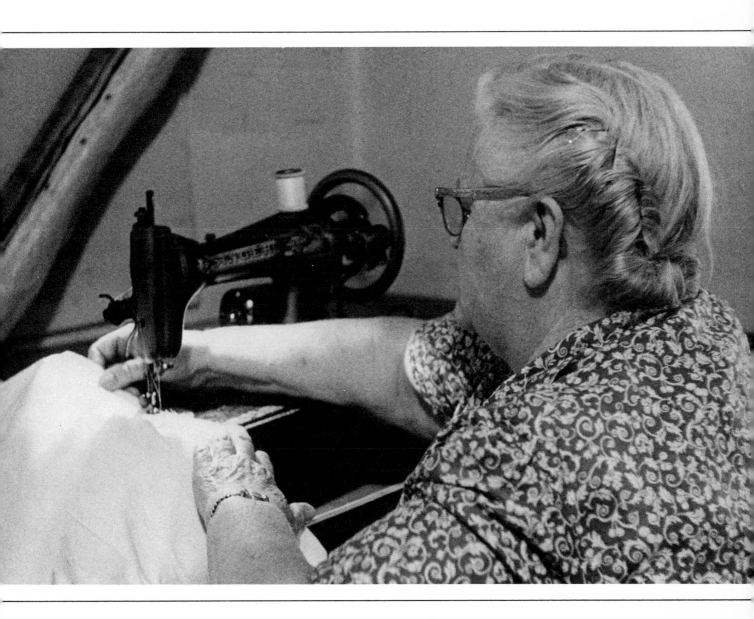

"If I ain't got social security, how can I live?"

"An elderly person is a person who has lost their background, lost their husbands or their wives in a great many cases, and they're dependent upon other people to give them a helping hand the rest of the road.

"I came from a moneyed family, and my mother cracked a mean whip. She controlled the money, and "You do as I say or else." Well, I wasn't buying that. So I went out determined to find my own way. I went into nurses' training, and I can never understand how I made it, but I did.

"I had fifty four years being married, and it was all very lovely. Then suddenly things began to break the other way. The husband died, and the daughter went off and got married and went on her own. And then all of a sudden, all contacts are lost, and you're a bit bewildered and bewitched, wondering just how to fill in the time that was filled in before. I filled mine in for thirty years working with blind people doing braille. Before that I did hand weaving. I've always kept busy, and then, all of a sudden, that's blank.

"It was utter devastation, because I knew what was wrong with my husband the year before he died. I knew he had cancer of the throat, and I found it very hard to face him, till finally he lost his voice. To me it was something that had to happen, but it was he who had faith in God. He said, "It's up to God." It took me nearly three years to realize this. I had it put very nicely to me. Pope Paul, President Kennedy, and my Jack, all died within a period of six months. So some friend of mine said, "God took all the good Johns at one time." I said, "He didn't need mine, I needed him." I can't go into it yet without weeping after eight years. We were very compatible. We travelled a great deal, we read a great deal, we entertained a great deal, and those are all the things that go to make up a satisfactory married life.

"I got a one room apartment, and I did a great many things. I filled in my days beautifully, and all of a sudden the picture was changed. The money started to run out, and the things weren't good. I had to come here, an old folks home for the poor. I have a new world. Believe me, it isn't easy to adapt to it. Anyone you talk to will tell you honestly the changeover is a big step. Mrs. Smith took the step from the eighth floor to the basement and said, "That's the longest step that I ever took." Well, that's me too. This is the longest step that I ever took. There's a sense of insecurity. There's just nothing to hang on to."

"My dollar is my relative. When I've got that, I've got everything.
If you haven't got that, you're in pretty bad shape."

"My husband left me plenty of money. Thank goodness I don't have to worry about that."

"Outside of my arthritis, I don't have no worries. I don't have to worry where my next meal is going to come from, and that means a whole lot. Uncle Sam is taking care of all his children with social security, and that goes a long way with your rent, your food. So what more? I'm happy."

"If I had watched my money better than I did, I'd of been better off than I am today. You've got to watch those things. You've got to learn those things when you're younger. I think if someone had told me to watch my money a little bit better, I'd be better off today. That's what the thing is. How can people live without money? When you're younger, you don't realize.

"Perhaps sitting in a big house with a lot of old things around, you're lonely just the same as me."

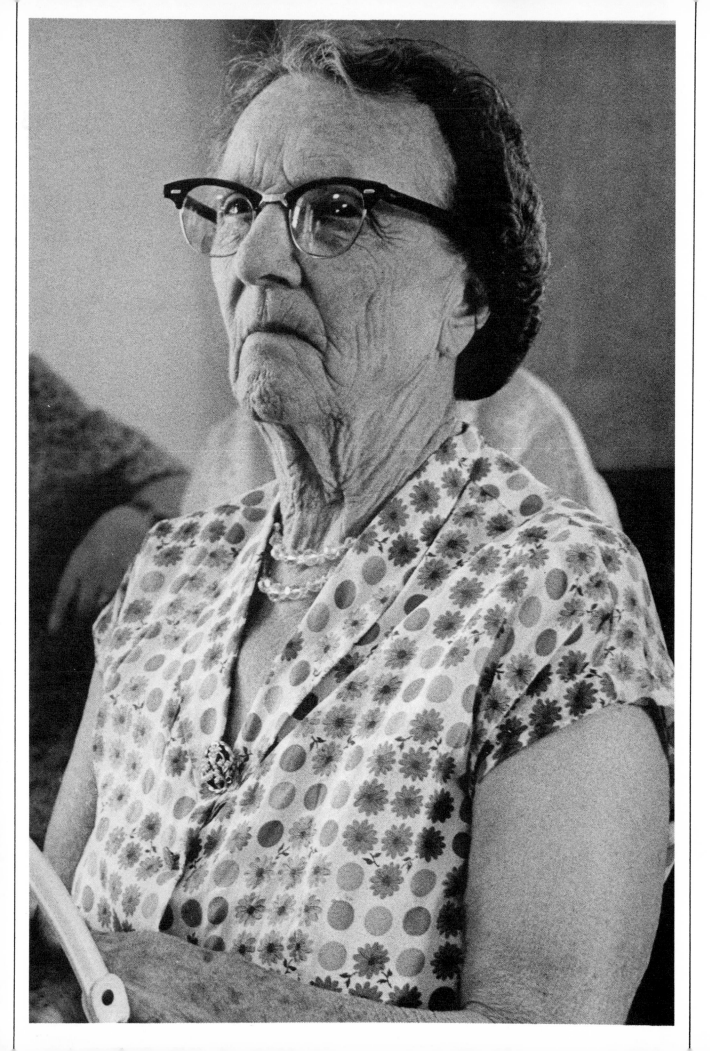

"Back when I couldn't get any money, I didn't have anything to buy anything with. Now I'm getting a little money, and stuff's so much higher than it was then, 'till it ain't so much different."

"We've always had problems, but it seems like the problems get worse the older you get."

"I think the biggest problem that has been with either one of us has been sickness. Ordinarily people after sixty, if they had the wherewithal, why that's the time that they travel, see the world, enjoy themselves, and do the many things they've worked for all their lives. Well, that's what we rather figured we'd do. We did do quite a little traveling, 'till my husband got sick. He hasn't been very well now for the last seven years, and I have a heart ailment that kind of keeps us from doing so many things that we'd like to do.

"My husband has been in the hospital now over eight months outside of twenty-six days. He's getting pretty well worn out with it all. . . . Some days he's pretty discouraged, but he hasn't lost the fight of it. It's just going to take time now. It isn't just one thing. He's had one thing after another.

"Just as soon as he is able, why he'll be back home again. It is lonely for me. It is extremely so. The evenings and the nights are more so. Of course I don't lay in the day. I'm up, getting ready to get over here. Then I go home. Half the time when I go home, I'm kind of tired and I lie down, sleep, rest or work on books.

"It seems we've had quite a time just helping ourselves. I just think that I've spread myself just as far as I can spread. Then I can see that my husband, he's getting better slowly. In a way it is discouraging. I sometimes feel like giving up, and then I just rest and get to think the matter over and decide to start all over again. I just don't think about going on. I just want to, want to live. I kind of like this old world. . . . He's just fighting now to get well enough to get up and go home."

"Old age is a nice time of your life, as long as you have your health."

"Well, I can't be happy because I'm sick."

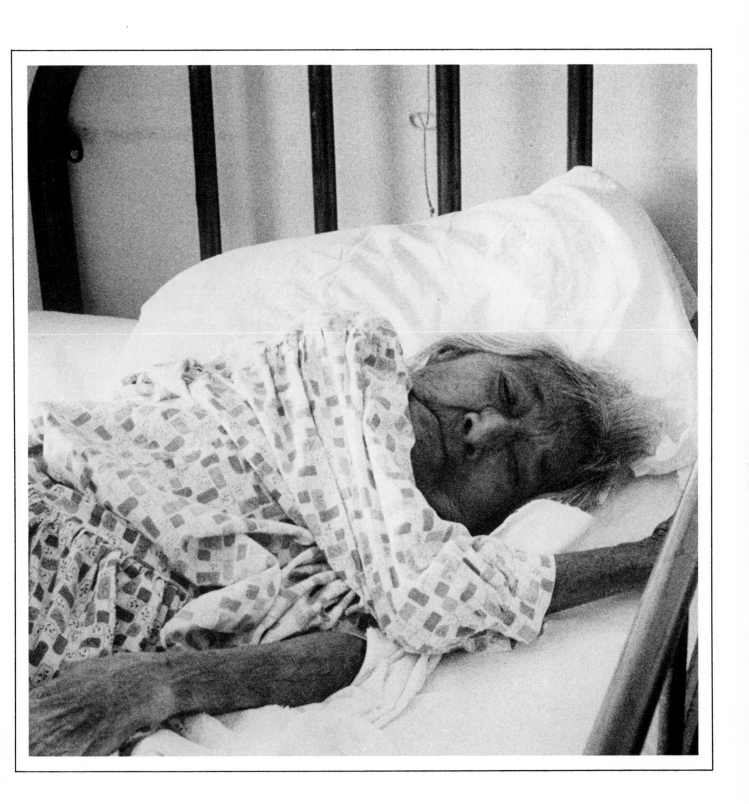

"I find you get ailments when you get older, unexpected ailments. If it's a heart ailment and you're told about it, it's a great shock. When it hits you, it's something like you never think it can happen to you. When it does happen to you, it shatters you for a while. After several weeks, maybe months, you get to realize, well, that nothing is going to do away with it, but you can probably lighten it with medication and doing what the doctor says.

"Like me, I've always had a lot of energy. I was just like something, if I'd stop I couldn't go any more. I'd just overdo it. Even though I still have a lot of energy, I have to stop. I realize it, and I do stop for a while."

"My spirits are all right, but I get depressed at times over my condition. . . . How uncomfortable it is. It's very frustrating and annoying. I can't do anything about it."

"With arthritis in my bones, I'm not the gadder I used to be."

"There's this old bat who is in a wheelchair. Even in a wheelchair, she's a real gadabout, but when she hears one of her kids is coming, she pretends to be all stove up with rheumatiz and her heart. Anymore she just complains how nobody cares whether she lives or dies, and she can't get around at all, and she's just waiting to die."

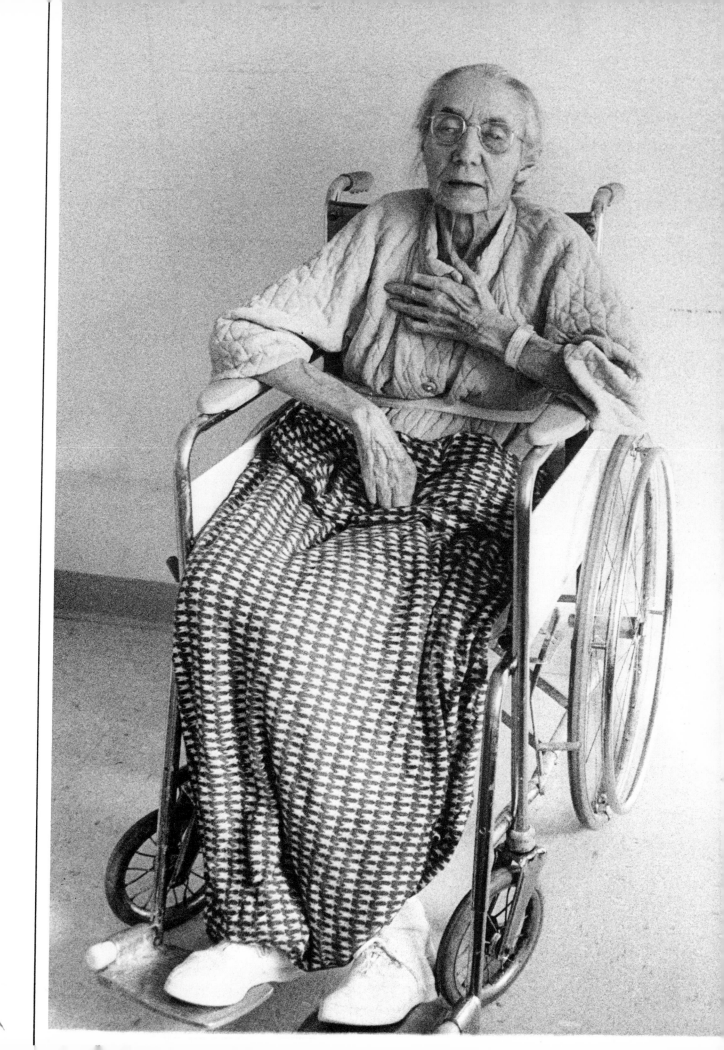

"If you're extremely active like I happen to be, sometimes you say, 'Oh, my God, come on. Pep it up a little bit', or something like that. You get a little pushy like you'd like to shake somebody because they don't have the same pep that you do."

"As you get to know your wife better and you have children together and raise them, you become more united—you become closer together over the years."

"Seems to me that marriage—I guess it's like old wine; it improves with age."

"It ain't like it used to be. Sometimes I want to be with a woman, but not very often. It changed when I got to be eighty years old. I'm eighty-four now. It's just not there."

"It seems that your husband is your best friend. If you're with him, you've got all your friends."

'I know what life is about now, what suffering is and struggle."

"When your husband dies, you start a whole new life."

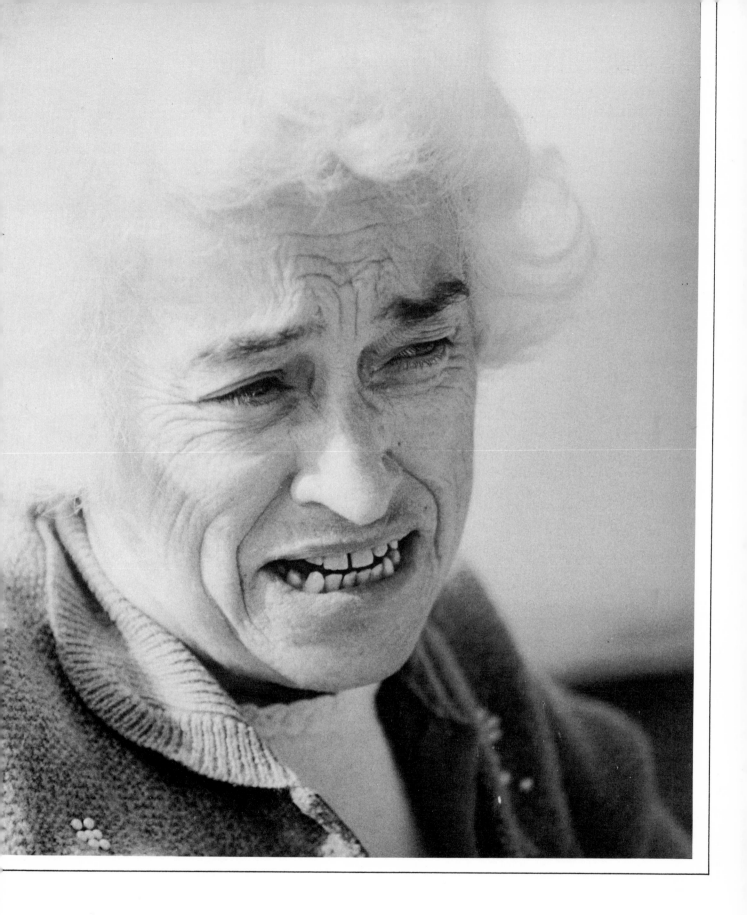

"Now there was my husband, he was eighty three. He was gettin' up there. He would come in and lie down on the couch a little while and maybe he'd start to snore; he'd be asleep. Well in a few minutes he'd wake up, "Well, I'd better get up and get busy." He got up the same way the day he died. He was laying on the couch and he got up, got his cap on, and took out towards the garden. Then he got his rake and went to raking up the leaves and trash. I guess he fixed him a little pile or something, and then set a match to it, and that was it. He caught afire so quick and burned up, that there's nobody that realizes. Nobody knows from that hour on, exactly what happened. . . . I never heard him make a sound. That woman next door, I heard her yell help, and I knew something was wrong. I just begin to get to that door as fast as I could, and of course then I realized it was Andy. I just didn't know what to do, and I was afraid to go out there, 'fraid I'd just be in the way and maybe fall and hurt myself, and then I'd be there to see about. First thing I knew, there was some lady came in and grabbed the telephone, and there's a great big feller come in and took the receiver from her. He sez, "Let me call." Well in the meantime she was asking me what number to dial, and it all happened so fast and so quick, till I didn't know what was going on hardly, thinking about him out there.

"Other people can't read your mind or your heart . . . That's it. So after all . . . there's mountains . . . and there's valleys . . . and all that goes in life. All I know to do is to be thankful to God. We can call on him and go to him in time of need and can read our Bible and pray . . . That's what helps us along. If it wasn't for that consolation, . . . there's a lot of times, I don't know what I'd ever done. I guess there's always a way. Though sometimes it seems awfully dark, and I don't know what you call it, but you know yourself, it's harder sometimes than it is others."

"A lot of old people remarry just for companionship. A lot of them get married in old age. It isn't more or less love. It's companionship. When you're younger, you can marry because there's love. When you're older, it's to have somebody around your house. If you're old and you have to do all your own cooking and washing and everything else, it gets kind of hard on you."

"Get married again? Who'd want to marry an old woman like me?"

"My grandchild says he can tell when people are old, because they don't smile. They're always sad."

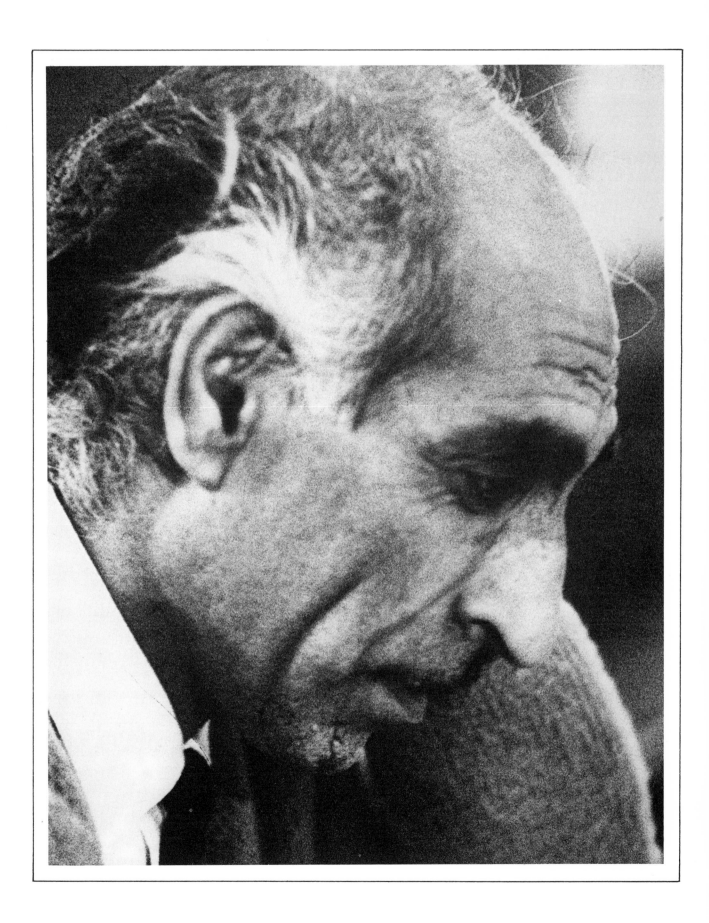

"When the dinner hour comes, I feel sorry for myself, and I'm not the only one. So sometimes I take the bus downtown and have coffee and dessert. As I said before, it's not being needed. That's the bugbear of all who are alone."

"It seems that when we're old is when we need our companions. I don't know, but it seems funny that our loved ones is gone, when we need them most, when we're getting up to the senior years."

"Living alone is a lonesome business."

"I found the cat at the door the first Christmas after my husband died. I think God sent him to me. He's been a blessing, a good companion."

"I like to watch the birds, the people coming and going, to think, relax, sleep sometimes, and I especially like to talk to my friends. We all try to meet at the same time in the afternoon."

"I want to be active and take part in things. I want to go to meetings or anything like a program or entertainment. This is why I really enjoy being with the senior citizens."

"I just like the senior citizen group as a whole. Some of them are my old acquaintances. They've known me pretty much all my life in a way. I like to plan for us to do things, have things. That's the main part I like. I offered my place, if they would put the building up so we could have a center. I'd lease my ground to them if they would build on it, because I couldn't build a building big enough. I really did offer that, because I like being with the group. I felt they'd be company to me coming in and out and knowing they were over there on my ground. I'd just enjoy it, 'cause see my mother's gone, and I didn't have no sisters, no brothers. I was the only child. It really left me alone, outside the children in a way, but they were just growing up. It wasn't like having someone kind of my age."

"I like the senior citizen center, because there is always something to do. You like to play cards, there's cards. There are pot luck dinners, anything you want."

"I can't sit still and die. I have to keep busy."

"I love children. I enjoy babysitting. They seem to like me, and I like them. They love me, and I love them. I can tell they love me because they're always coming and getting up in my lap and hugging and kissing me. I don't have no grandchildren. I call 'em my children, and sometimes they call me 'mama.' "

"My wife says that she's our little masterpiece."

"I felt my greatest joy when I first touched my grandchild."

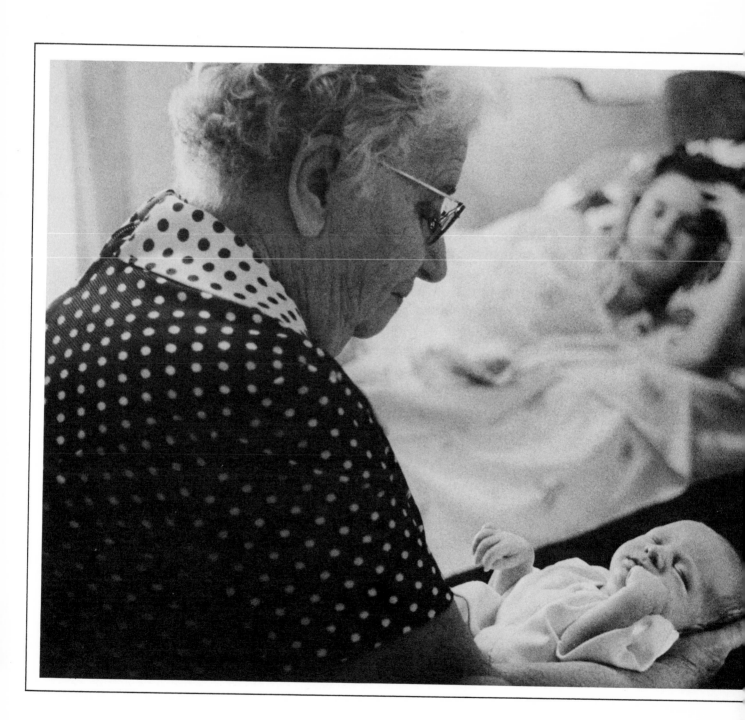

"Well, in some ways I'm living better now, but when I had my children around 'bout me, I believe that was the happiest time of my life. When I had my little children all around me, that was wonderful times, and my husband. Maybe we didn't have a lot of the modern conveniences. Now when my husband and I started out, you know we've been, you might call us poor, and a lot of times where we lived we didn't have electricity, and at times we didn't have the telephone. But I think that was about the happiest time in my life, when I had my little family around me."

"I don't want to live with nobody. I want to be alone by myself. They ain't goin' put no headrag on my head and sit me in the corner and make me take care of them chilen. I'm not goin' do it. I'm absolutely not goin' stay with them."

"I sit around expecting somebody to visit me. I'm useless now. I can't work. I get lonesome sometimes here by myself. Sometimes my daughters come in and my boy come in. I feel better when they visit me. They care for me and visit me. That's all I'm happy about."

"You can't actually live with your people, because you feel like you're in the way. Perhaps you want to go to bed early, and they don't want to. You feel like you're in the way. It used to be that folks had old grandma living with them. They'd respect her and try to do what she wanted. It's not that way now. Old grandma has to sit in the background. They don't respect older age like they used to. Why I've seen the times, when they'd rather do anything than hurt their own grandma or grandpa, but now she's got to do what they think or say."

"I don't feel my relatives should be responsible for me. I want to be independent—just don't want to have to depend on anybody else."

"I don't want to live alone. When you live alone you talk to yourself. I'd want a companion, someone to live with me."

"I don't ever want to leave my own place. That's where all my things are that I've been keeping through the years. That's where I want to be."

"When a woman lives by herself, relatives are very important. My sister is especially important to me. Others just say, 'Here comes that old woman again.' "

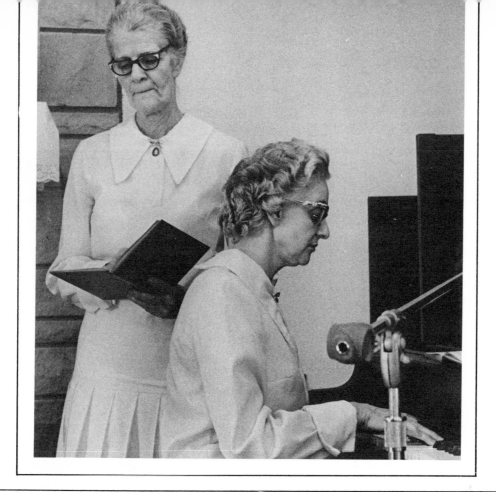

"I have plenty of people say, 'What do you want to keep those dogs for?' I tell them that I like those dogs. They're just something that's living. As long as you've got something you're interested in that's living, you're a lot better off."

"You're old, when you own a pet. That's when your grandchildren have grown too old to bother with you."

"Yes, I do get lonely. When I feel like it, I go to my neighbor's and sit on the porch with her. Usually we go to the auction together every week."

"What is life without friends?"

"I'm not too anxious to mingle with people my age. They just talk about aches and pains."

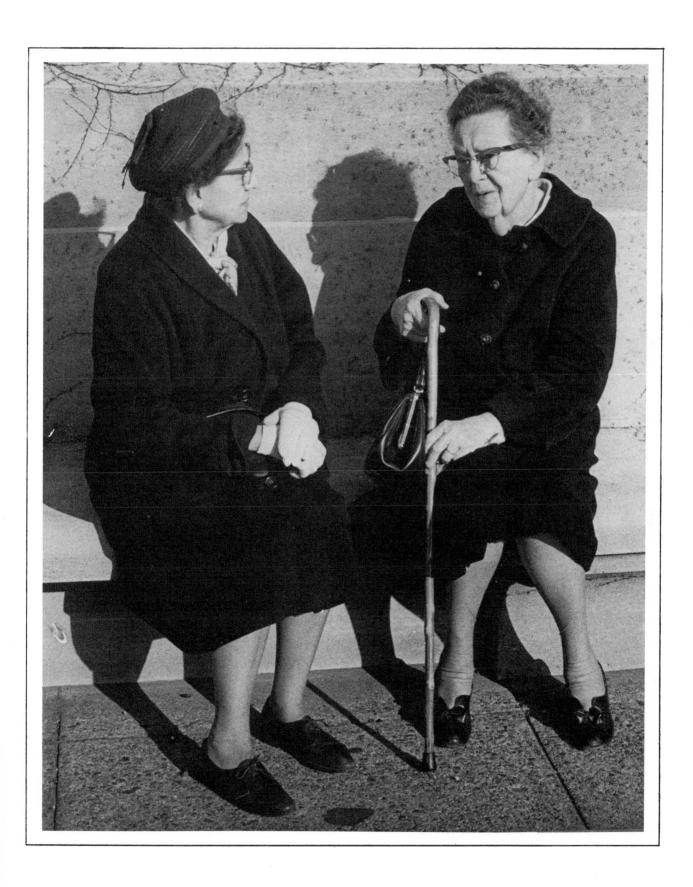

"When people get older, they cling together more."

"So many old friends drift away and into the cemetery."

"We had lived in this little town for thirty-six years, and the friends that I had, had died. I just buried a lot of my good friends. Every time I went to a funeral, I felt bad. It's a changing in a phase of your life, that's passed on."

"It breaks your heart to see your friends die. As you get older, you think about it more and wonder when it's your turn. The day two people died, I couldn't go to the second graveyard. I went to the funeral; I had to, but I just couldn't go to the second one."

PART II

"I heard a doctor who deals with older people saying, 'You just can't kill them off.' I think that's true. We just keep living on and on and on."

"The thing about getting older is that you get more experience about life, and you can advise the younger people."

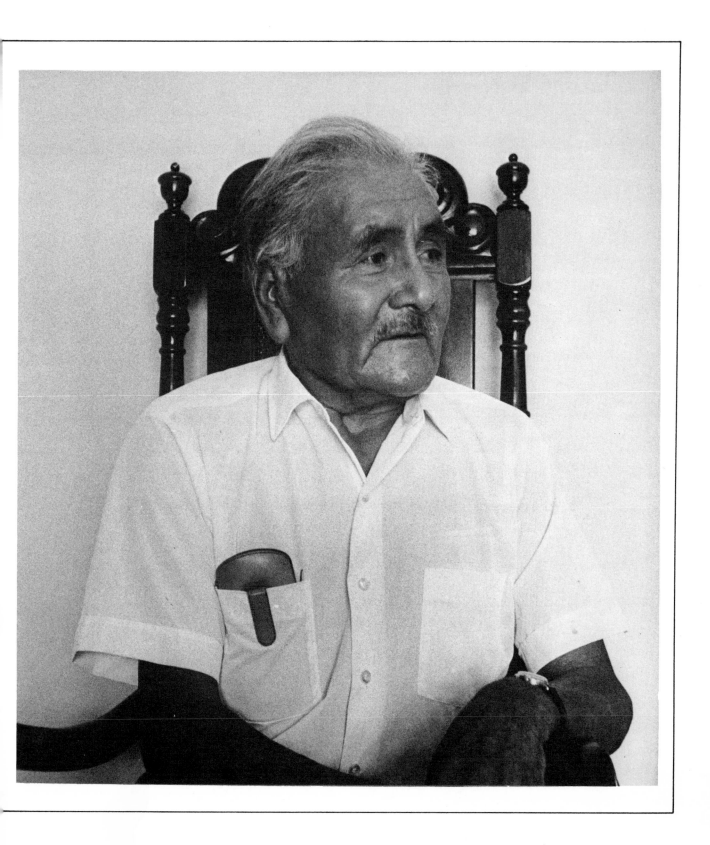

"You can not think otherwise than respect an aged person."

"I feel like I've done my part. I do have the feeling that I have some accomplishments under my belt, and I can look back on those with satisfaction. I'm interested in what goes on, but another generation has taken over now. I'm perfectly glad for them to do it."

"I like to be among younger people, and I think they're great. It's a new generation, and they can cope with things that have been done wrong by the older people."

"I figure we've had our chance. I had about forty good years and had the experiences of life. It's time to let the young folks carry on. I don't feel resentful, because if I muffed those forty years, that's my hard luck. If you weren't successful in forty years, why keep on?"

"I can't understand a college man with everything, having hair so long that you can't tell the difference between him and her. A HIPPIE. A hobo was a good man in my day. He was a gentleman. He wanted something to eat, not to destroy like they do today. I think it's a disgrace."

"I ain't got anything in the world to do with it, but I don't like the way the young folks fix their hair, either the way they wear their clothes. I don't like it, but I have to take it, because I can't help it. They work when they want. When they don't want, they don't do nothing. I'm thankful the Lord put them here, but I don't worry about them. But what they wear! I don't like nothing they wear. I ain't got nothing to do with it. I just go on. Thank God they don't go naked."

"I've been traveling. Last five months I've been down the coast from Portland, Maine to New York, Philadelphia, Baltimore, Raleigh, and right on down to the Keys.

"I come from a broken home. My father died, when I was about eight years old. No home life. The old lady, God bless her, had no responsibility. She threw me in a home and visited me once a month, but I don't hold that against her. That woman had a lot of misery. The old man, drunken, he died of acute alcoholism. So I'm like father, like son.

"I never hit skid row. I take care of myself. I keep looking good. I've lost more clothes through drinking, beautiful clothes. I'd get them, and I'd lose them. I try and stay in better places. I usually have a little place to stay in a hotel. I check in a hotel a couple of days, then check out. You never know where you're going to wind up when you're drinking.

"I'm just getting off a drunk now. I'll look better in a couple of days when I stay off that booze. My eyes clear up. I look beautiful and start to take care of myself. Look like a real wheeler dealer. After you drink so much, your reflexes begin to slow down too. A couple of times you get that real fearful feeling. It's a cold terror. I guess everybody's had it.

"Now, I just want to settle down in a small place. Get a few bucks. Get a lot of dust. Settle down. Take care of business. Lay around the house. I'd be happy."

"I'm very disappointed in the youth of today. Well, their lack of thought and the moral standard that is being reduced to the extent that it is. It's going to have a terrific effect on the future generation. This country is just going down, down, down. Anybody will tell you that."

"One of the things that upsets me more than anything else is the lack of appreciation of some of our citizens for the privilege of being an American. This feeling that government owes them something, but they owe nothing to the government—I go on crusades about that. To me, God blessed those of us whose people sought America's shores, and we owe the United States of America a great deal. I hope never to be so busy that I can't serve. I work in Veterans' Hospitals, and I work in various organizations with one aim, and that is to help those who have served America."

"I've been fighting against war for all these years. You can never gain anything by destruction. You can gain only by building. When you're advocating war, you're advocating destruction."

The Selling of the
Candidates for a
Republican Senate.....

$100 MILLION PLUS!

Apply to Pres. NIXON
and Vice-Pres. AGNEW.

ELECTION STRATEGY:

Forget the War... Just Pay
the Bill... $60 Million Daily!
O.K.?

"Frankly, I think a person who steps on an American flag should be tried and put in jail for punishment. I don't approve of rioters looting a store or this breaking and entering. We have laws to take care of people like this, and there's no excuse for any American citizen doing it. I don't believe any of these fine tales of they have the privilege of deciding which wars they fight in. If the United States is committed, all of us are committed."

"Oh, I think the world has changed a whole lot. Oh, worse, but I. . . .
I don't know. Sometimes I think it'll get better, but we have such a
difficulty in people doing things that I don't think they should do, like
using that dope and drinking. Then there's so much holding up. I'd say
the people that are able to work, they ought to get out and work like
us people did in our days."

"We were living in Denver, and there were just three white people left in the whole block. We had to get out. We had a beautiful home there. I had forty two different kinds of roses. I just had everything you could think of. We lived right on the corner, and we had great big windows and was afraid that a brick would come through. Next door to us there was a young boy seventeen years old. He was a nice kid, and he never had a bunch down there raising the devil or anything. He walked half a block down the street, and someone shot him in the head and killed him. Three doors from us, there's just a whole lot of broken down cars; so we just moved.

"When I left Denver, I had over two hundred African violets. Of course I had to give up all of those, and I gave away a lot of other things. Oh I could just kick myself. I thought I wasn't going to last here, and what's the use of hanging on to it? A revolver I'd dragged around for fifty years and two beer mugs that I'd dragged around for fifty years. Now as long as I'm here, I don't say they would be any good to me; they'd just sit there, but I'd like to have them. You know, my pajamas, my sheets, my pillowcases, and everything I've got.

"Now it's dangerous to stick your nose out at night. It really is. I won't even walk to town in the daytime. I never used to lock my door at night, but now I stay locked in, even in the daytime. Isn't that terrible?"

"Times has changed. That makes a great difference between the young people and the old people, 'cause they've got their way, and we've got our way. They feel their way is right, and we feel our way is right, which we know because we've experienced it. We're older than they are. We've come over the road that they've got to come over. The young people now tell you that you don't know. Some of them say that this is the Atomic Age, and we don't know what the Atomic Age is. We older people don't know in a way, because we haven't experienced it. So most naturally we don't know. We just see life different, and this is a different age. I know it's a different age. I feel it. I feel it in mind, and I feel it in body."

"We were a pioneer family from Nebraska. We lived on the farm, ten children; three pairs of twins. My father helped lay the first railroad in Nebraska for the Union Pacific. He said that there were so many Indians around that he thought it would never be settled up. So he went back to Illinois; that's where he came from. Then he and mother were married. Seven years later they came back to Nebraska and homesteaded. Forty acres was all they could get because the rest of it had all been taken in that seven years. That was not very much land with such a large family, but father was very industrious, and he did real well in the purebred stock business."

"I remember the days when they used to plow with oxen and went in wagons and buggies, but the most of the people would walk. Now people don't want to walk noway. I used to walk to town and tote groceries back. We people, all of us, white and black, had it pretty hard.

"Now we is going to school and learning, and you can go to church all the time if you want to. Well, it's a change. Young folks can't see it like us, but we can see the change, feel it, know it; see the change of the world. Great change have took place and is gradually takin' place stronger and stronger."

"Things have changed quite a bit you know. Cause I wanted to go to school and get an education. I wanted to be a music teacher, so I could help myself.

"My mother and my father separated when I was very small, and my mother worked in taking care of us. When I got up sixteen years old, I just felt that my mother was getting up in the age, where she couldn't work and send me to school like I wanted to. I wanted to go to Booker T. Washington School. Where I got to the place where I could quit school, well I did.

"I went working in a glass factory in East St. Louis when I was sixteen years old. There's where I stayed a good while, and then I left there and went to the packing house. I stayed there 'till we left East

St. Louis and came here. I worked down here in the furniture factory and then I went out to private homes. Now I can't do none of that. I wouldn't try to go to a house and get a job, because I don't think I could stand up under that work.

"Children that go to school, they got a way that they can work part time and go to school part time. When I was coming up, they didn't have that. The university now will take and lend children money to go to school, and then they can work and pay that back. The children have it so much easier now, than they did when I was coming up.

"I've worked awful hard all my life, so I think now is kinda the time for me to take it easy. I don't take it as easy as I should because my husband is sick. He's getting worse and worse all the time. He's not getting any better. That makes it kinda hard on me. I have to watch him. I do my own work; my washing, ironing, housework. I have to do all the running, going shopping and everything.

"My health is not so good now because I have high blood pressure. The doctor said I should take it easy, but I can't take it easy. Well, you get sickness in the house. You see my husband's been sick about twelve, fourteen years."

"Born in Poland, in Europe. Came here 1913 before the first War. In Poland, I work on a little farm. Is good. Then father died. My brother he not work on the farm. Oh, my God, got trouble. Nothing to eat. That's why I come over here. My cousin didn't want to go into the Polish army. So my cousin and me come over here. The first war, he take in the army over here.

"Here I come 1913. 1917 depression come. In week sometime make two dollar, five dollar, nothing to work. I look into the window until I cry. My goodness. Poor in Poland. Poor over here.

"Married here. Man very good but didn't make nothing. I work, senior thread and button maker.

"My husband died. Nobody bring the pay. My son fourteen. Tax to pay. Insurance. I have to work all the time. Too old to work now. I get job. Doctor say quit job. Is too much on eyes.

"I come to hotel. Seven o'clock, get up. Breakfast. In the morning I help put dishes in the kitchen. Listen television. Dinner time. Sit. Supper time. Watch T.V. night sometime after supper. Go to bed."

"Really I've lived from the oxcart days to the man in the moon. Since 1900, let's face it, America has had a great number of tremendous things happen, advances in science, medicine, and all those things."

"And we just keep living on and on and on."

PART III

"When you get over sixty-five or seventy, that's a second childhood. You're stubborn just like a child, and you opinionate so hard. A child when it's born, he doesn't hear, he doesn't see, he doesn't walk. When you get old, you become the same way. Your hearing starts to fail. Your eyesight, everything fails. . . ."

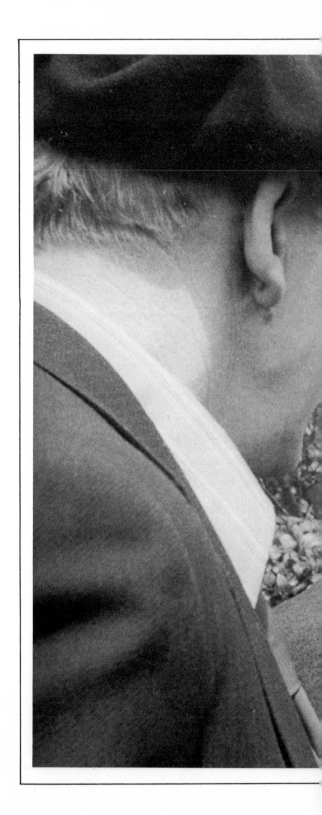

"We have a good time here at the pool, dunking and pulling under. We say, 'Oh, this senile bunch down here. They're in their second childhood and all that.' We kid a lot about that."

"I don't worry so much anymore. I guess I ain't trying to do things like I used to. I guess I got so as I know."

"It's a process of getting older. You don't get older fast, but you know that you're going to get older. You begin sharing more with one another; sitting, talking, knowing that you don't have something big on hand that you have to do."

"When you get older, you get a little wiser and become a little more tolerant. You don't see things in black and white. You learn to compromise."

"My religious beliefs have made my older years happy."

"The older people grow and the closer they get to dying, the more likely they are to take up religion. They get too old to sin, so they take up religion."

"When I was working, I couldn't go to church every day. I had to work during the day, and the only time I could go was on Sundays. Now I go to mass every day. It makes me feel better. As you get older, you want to spend more time in the chapel and in prayer. Your time gets shorter. It just comes natural to me."

"Old age is just something that we all have to face. The children of Israel, when they started out of Egypt into the promised land, they started on a great trip. Well, we too are doing that each day of our lives as we get a little bit older. We're on a journey. We're not going to stop at some promised land in this world. It's a promise to each and every one of us that lives the right kind of life. I feel that if we live the right kind of life, someday the land we'll go to, there'll be no sickness, sorrow, pain, or death. All of this will soon be gone."

"I don't have no way to get to church."

"Oh yeah, I still go to church. I like it more, but when you get up in age, you don't feel like dressin'. I really love to dress. Then folks don't pay attention to you being old. Put on your white clothes and they won't be looking at the ole lady. They be looking at how dressed up you is."

"Well, in some ways, I'm a whole lot happier, a different happiness. I just feel happy, spiritually happy."

"I'm thankful to God that I'm here."

"Partial solitude doesn't bother me. I like to be with people, but sometimes I like to be alone, to read and work in the garden. We all change with age, and that change is so slow from year to year that we can not follow it. We get more from quietness as the years go by."

"I think we like more and more quiet. We enjoy the peace and the quiet. In the evenings, it's beautifully quiet. It's just delightful to listen to the silence. It's just beautiful."

"The principal part of my life today is memory. There haven't been many bad things in my life, except disappointment in not being able to accomplish more."

"At night, if I can't sleep, I'm always thinking of the past. They're mostly unpleasant things. I came from a large family. I was next to the youngest, and my mother died when I was just a child. Well, the older girls and boys married and left me and the one next to me with the bag to hold. So I don't think I ever was a girl in a way. Of course as time went on, I got to dating and things like that, then everything began to change. I think I've had a very nice life. When I can't sleep at night, that's about the only time, I think about those things. During the day when there's so many other things to listen to and to do, those things don't bother me."

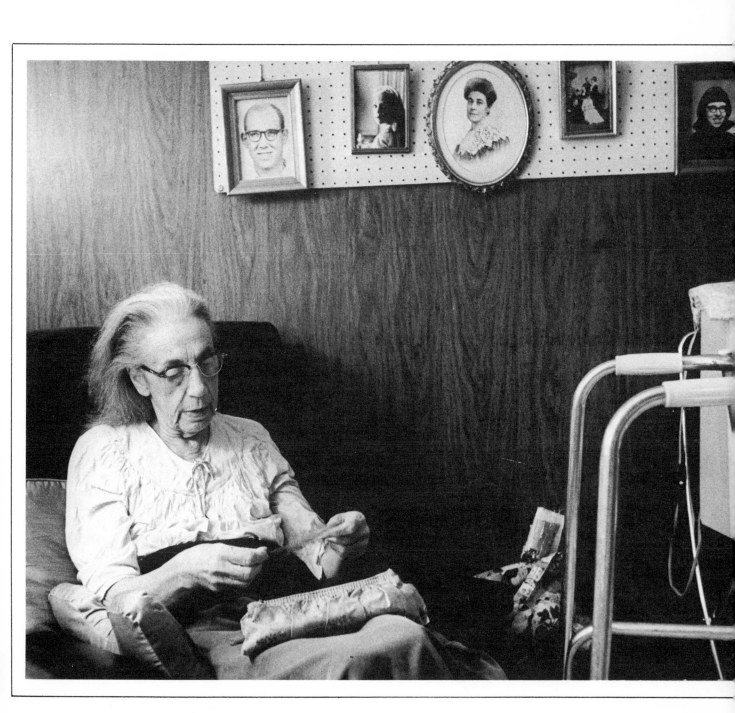

"After you get a certain age, you build up a backlog of very pleasant or unpleasant experiences. I like to remember the pleasant experiences that I've had. I like to remember my associations with my childhood, my home life—my parents, my early friends, and I like to remember that I have friends now."

"I don't feel old inside. I'm still as young inside as if I was in the twenties. But now when it comes to doing anything much anyway, your body won't take it. That's the only difference. I feel like I could go out and sing."

"I don't think of myself as getting older, though I feel a little older since I broke my hip. I do the washing, ironing, cooking, and housekeeping. My daughter works. Doctor says I'm fine."

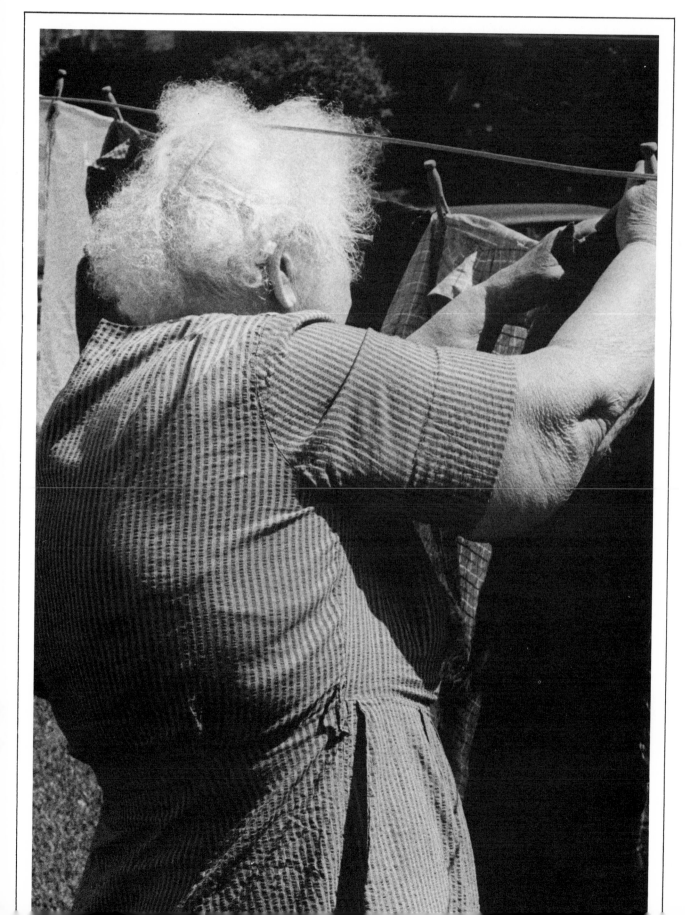

"Getting old is finding out that you can't do the things that you used to do. I used to start in the morning and do my work, and maybe help someone else. Now I'm beginning to find that I'm getting tired before I get all my work done. You can see my house. Not very clean. It makes you feel bad to see that your strength is not up to par."

"I wouldn't know how to tell you how it is to get old. When you want to do something, you can't. You remember when you was a little kid and wanted to do something, and you couldn't because you was too little. Then all of a sudden, you get big enough that you could. That's the way it is with everything, and it just goes on. Maybe some year your joints gets decrepit and things like that. I don't know how a person could tell you, you get old."

"I hate to talk about myself. I never liked old people in my life, and now that I'm old, I hate myself."

"What can older people offer? Practically nothing."

PART IV

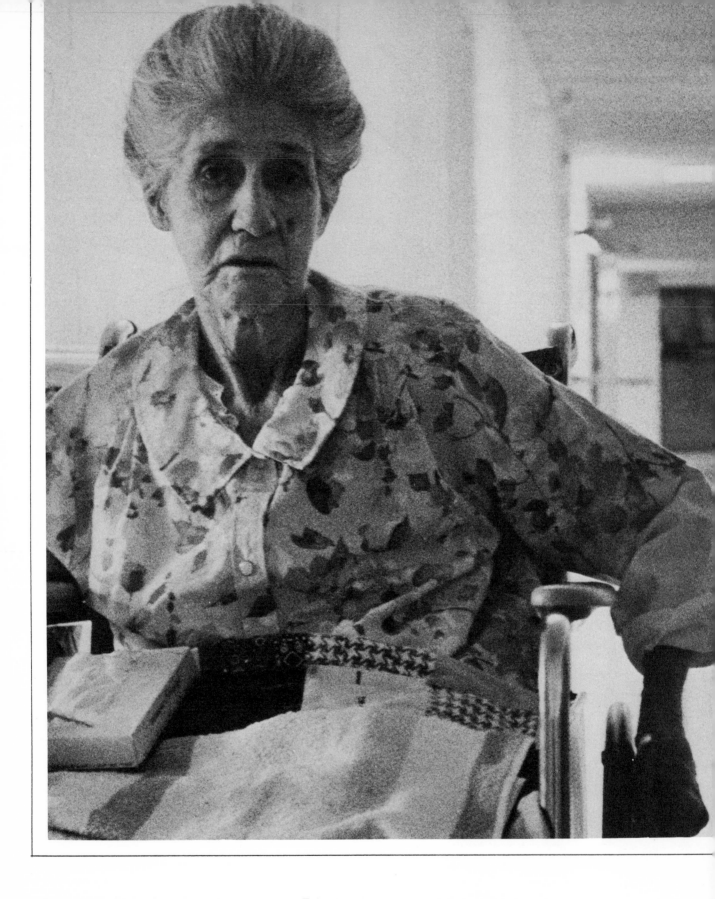

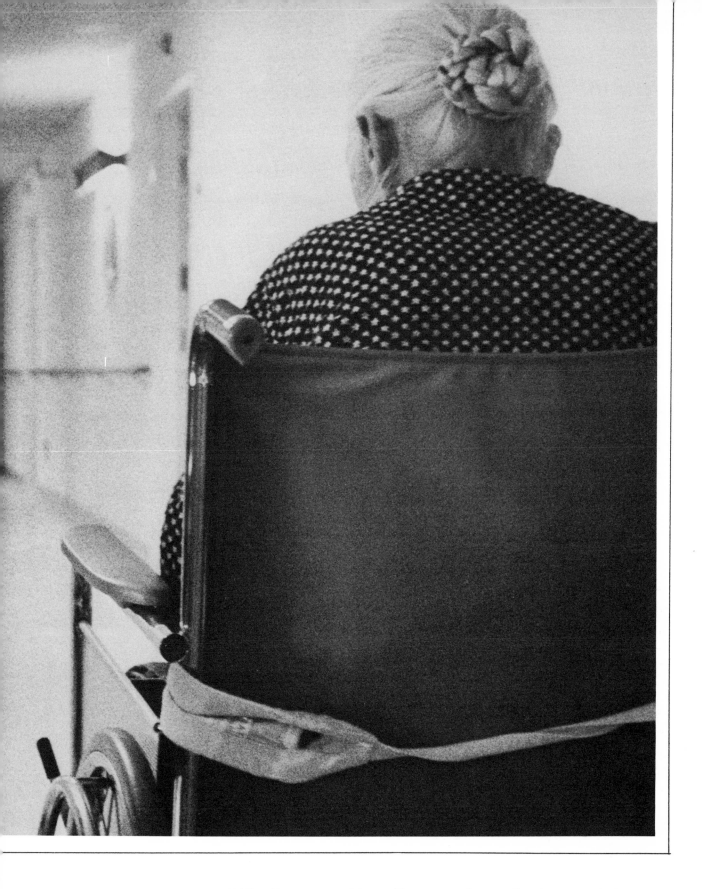

"I'll tell you one thing—I'm not going to live in any of those rest homes, and I'm not going to live with my daughters. I have a small income."

"The Indian raised his children, so that when he gets old, they ought to take care of him like he took care of them when they were small babies. He wants that in return. It's changing now. We have hospitals, and if a person gets sick like me at my age where I'm useless, well they take me to the hospital, and after a while they take me to a home."

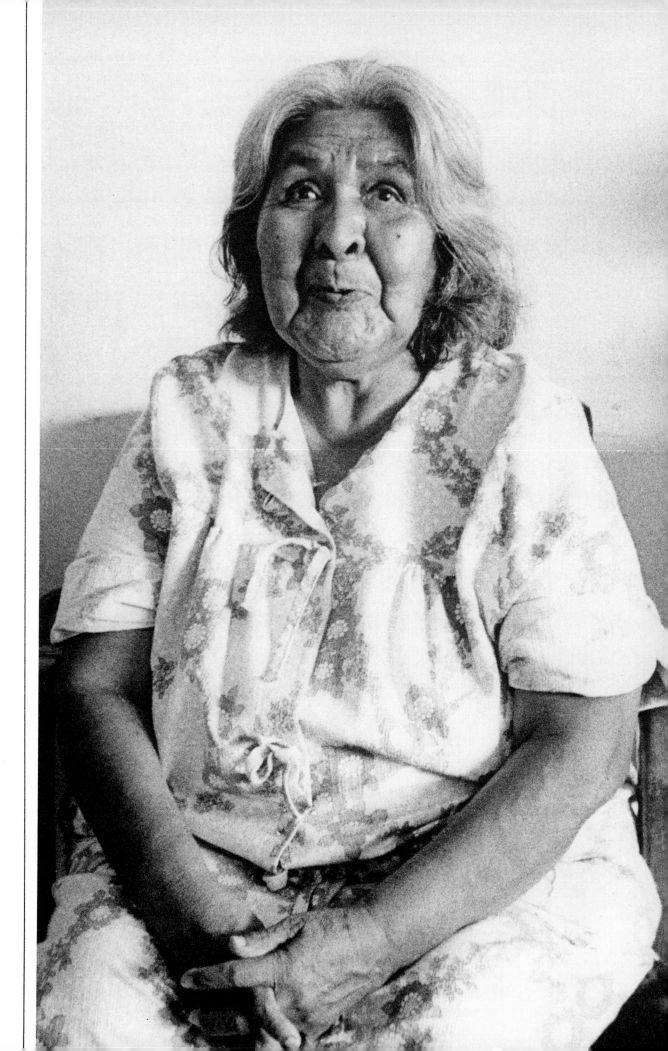

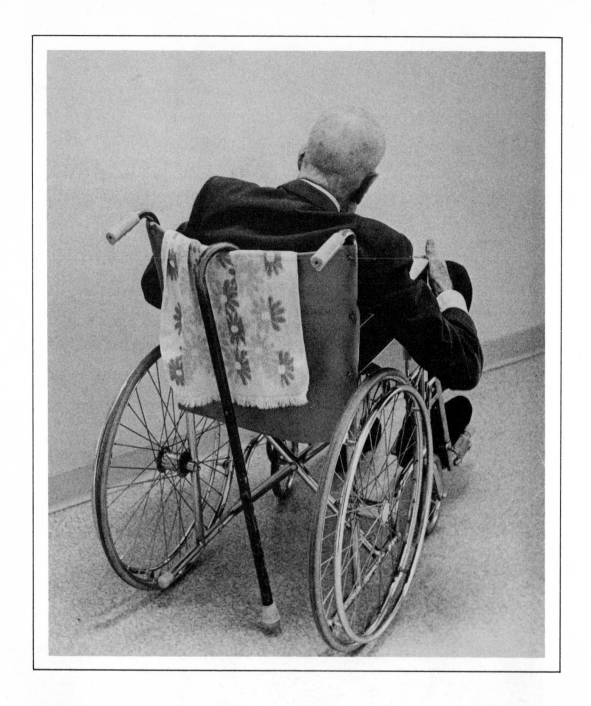

"They're actually a warehouse for old people."

"I know some nursing homes that I wouldn't mind being in. It's the way they're outfitted. Some of them don't feed the people right and don't take care of them."

"From what I have seen of them, I think they're pretty nice. Of course, I don't approve of them taking all of the old people's money."

"The lady that lives across the way from me, they took her mother to a nursing home. Now the old lady's begin to realize where she's at. Her daughter went down to see her and said they had gave her beans for supper. Now you know that's not a diet for an old person to have."

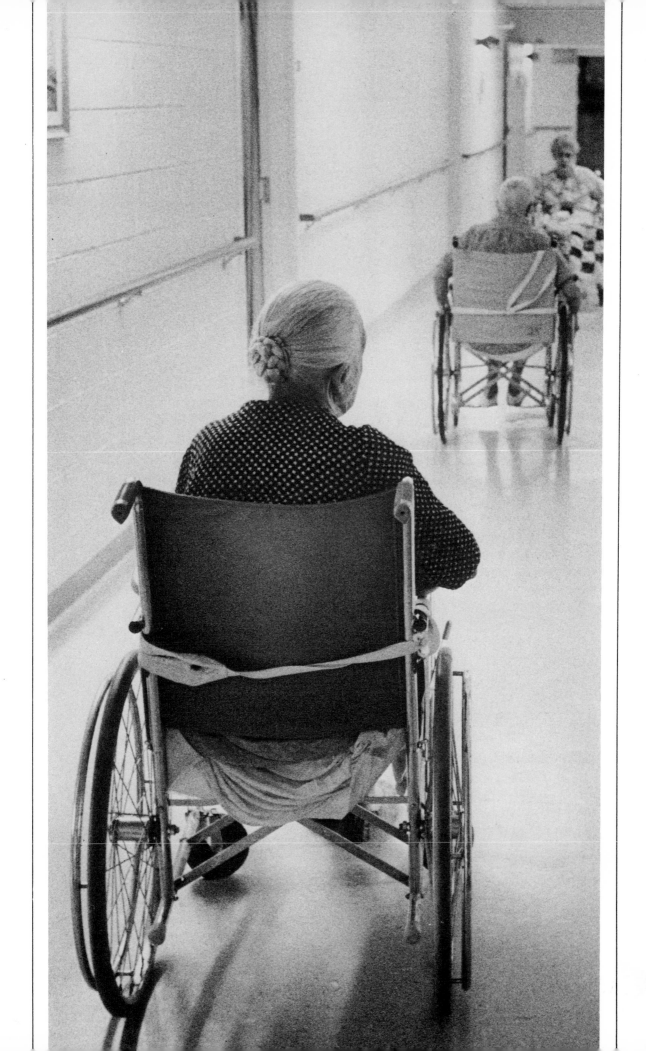

"At one time I thought about if I could get into one of the old folks homes, I would go into it. As far as a clean place, a well-kept place for people, why I'd rather go there than to stay here in my home and get way, just way out of condition. I have seen older people to get in that condition. It begins to kinda worry me, and I think, where would I go?

"I visited a home the other day, and it was so nice. One of the first things crossed my mind. I wondered if things got worse, would I be eligible to go to that home? I'd rather go in a home then be found here in this place."

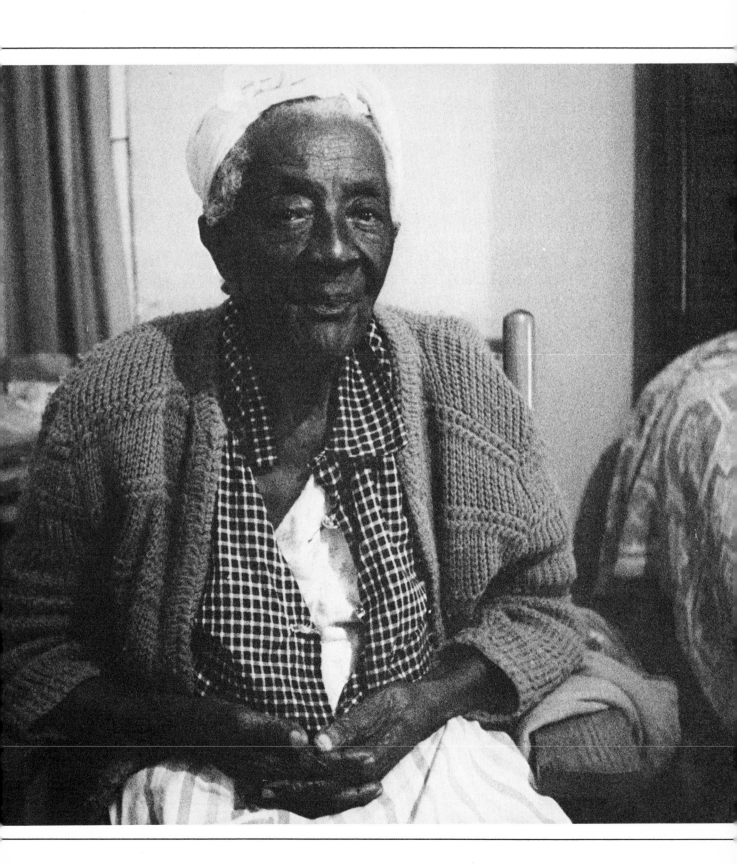

"I think a rest home is a fine thing when a person ain't got nobody to take care of them. I think that's a fine place for them to be put. I've been there to visit, and it look like I see them getting on very well. I went to see a friend up there in the hospital, and there was an old fellow in there. He was praying and wished he could get home. He said, Lord, I wish I was home. Yet I ain't got nobody to take care of me. After I left him, I went to see this other fellow. I said, Bud, you're in a nice, clean place. You ought to be happy here. Do you eat anything? He said, Oh, you ought to be here a little bit longer to see that tray when it come in here. Yeah, Man, I get all I want to eat, and they clean up nice. I think there couldn't be no better place than that for the older people when they ain't got nobody to care for them."

"I lived in a trailer house for fifteen years. I fell, and they all got excited. It didn't hurt me a particle, just fell down. Then my sister-in-law came around and put me in the hospital and called three doctors, just because I fell down. I haven't got over being mad at her yet. Oh, she comes here to see me. She brings me stuff."

"I don't know why I'm here. . . . Help me."

"Oh Lord, yes I feel low. Sometimes my mind leaves me."

"Why take an old person and stick needles in them and prolong life? Let nature take its course."

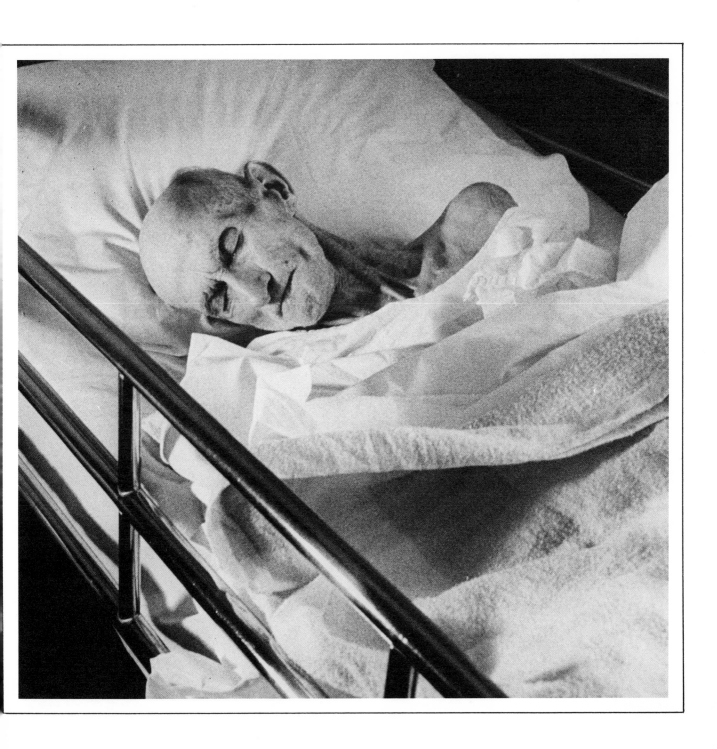

"When you get along past the seventies, you have to learn to live with a lot of things."

"I feel fine. . . . My birthday is the ninth of March, and I'll be one hundred. I lived a good life. God just wants me to live a bit longer. I certainly do want to live a little longer. I haven't given up yet. I don't use glasses. I've read the Bible through from Genesis to Revelations. I read it every night before I go to bed. That's a good book to read.

"My father and my grandfather were both soldiers in the War Between the States. My father was captured at the Battle of Gettysburg and was imprisoned for two years. His father was in the war too. They said that was right unusual, father and grandfather.

"I live here by myself. I don't mind it. I have a student that stays upstairs. I tell you I get my own breakfast and my lunch, and my daughter sends me a hot supper. I enjoy that supper. I read most all day. I have a girl that comes and kind of cleans for me, and I kind of dust around and help her some. . . . I belong to several things, like the Presbyterian church.

"Some days my daughter goes off with her husband. He has to go off a good deal. She goes with him, and I get mighty lonely when they go off.

"I had a fine husband. I guess the best thing I did was when I married him. I've been thinking about him so much today. . . . I think about him every day in the world. I lived with him fifty seven-years. We had our fifty years together. I miss my husband. . . . of course, that's the only thing.

"When my husband first passed away, my daughter said something about my living with her. I said, "No, Honey, I'm going to stay here in this house. This is my home. He built the home for me. I don't usually find myself too lonesome. My home means a lot to me. Of course, I don't keep it as well as I might.

"There are differences since I've gotten older. I don't walk so good. My daughter has to take me to have my hair fixed. . . . I don't approve of the young people today. They wear too short dresses. I go downtown, I go to a church meeting, I see more knees than anything.
  "I don't know how long I'll live. My health's good. I've just had this little trouble that I don't walk well. . . . I've enjoyed living so long."

"After you get on the other side of seventy-five, why there's not too much to do. Just take it easy."

"Yes, Effie sleeps a lot. She's ninety-six. She can't see, and she can't hear good. She lives in the past. She'll talk to me, and she knows I can remember back sixty-five years ago. She'll say, "Well Fred, do you remember so and so," and she'll bring up a story or a character and ask me do I remember a certain person. Then she'll speak of some incident of her and this other party doing something together. Once in a while we get wound up on something like that, and it's an interesting morning or evening or whatever.

"I try and read to her. It's almost impossible, because I have to read so loud. She don't hear. She won't worry about hearing aids. She just won't invest that kind of money. She says there's no point in buying eye glasses because she can't see anyway."

"I don't worry about dying, but I do think about it so hard. I don't mind dying, but you got to lay out there in the cemetery so long. That's what I hate. You gotta just lay there, forever and eternal. If I could just die and get up, it'd be all right, but I got to lay down and watch the roots."

"Old people are constantly bedeviled by a question that they can not get rid of, and that is, How long must we make ourselves last?"

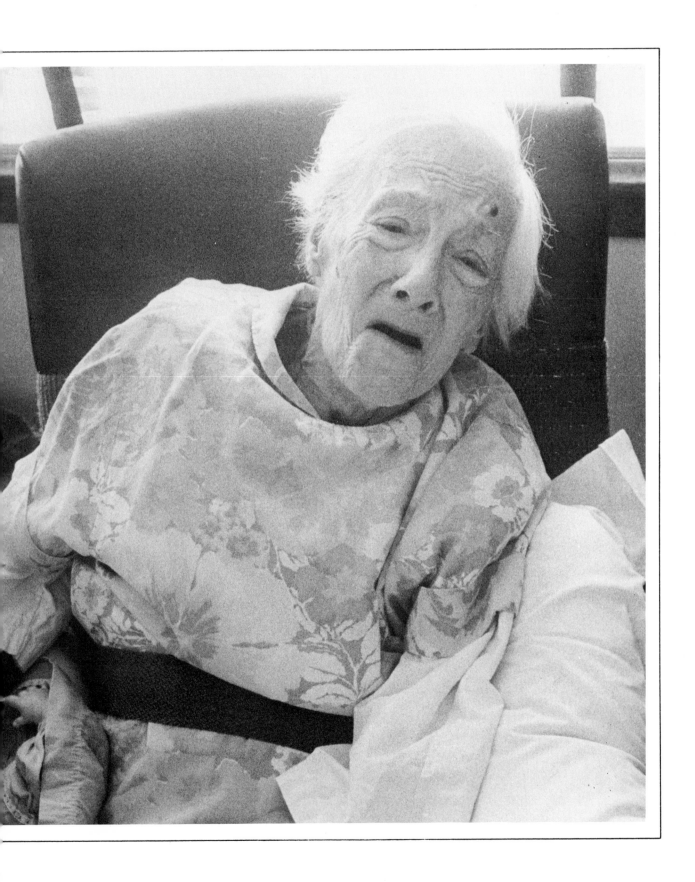

"Everybody's going to die. God didn't fix it where it worry you. He didn't fix it where you know when you going to die. If he had-a fixed it where you know you going to die, it might worry you. He didn't fix it that way. We don't know nothing about it. So that's the way it go.

"You're likely to die any time when you're old. Don't worry about that. I know what's going to happen. You jus' be gone. Somebody else got to take over where you were. Them that's living got to take over."

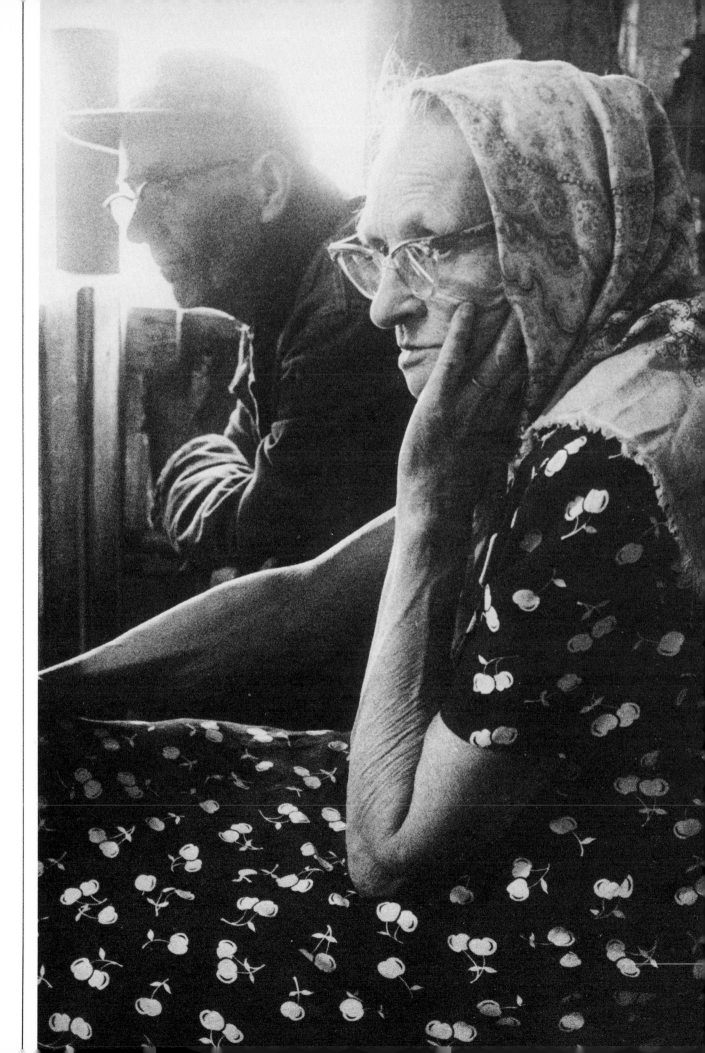

"We are here to end our days."